Take My Hand
Walk With Me

A collection of selected poems

1995 to 2018

Rickey K. Hood

UniqueVerses Publishing

Published by UniqueVerses Publishing
District Heights, Maryland

ISBN #0-9678457-6-9

Take My Hand Walk With Me *is a collection of new and selected poems spanning from the years of 1995 to 2018. This book is a collection of poems taken from previous small chapbooks:* ***In a little corner of a black man's mind stand I..., Tempes****t,* ***A heart's song sung to a friend,*** *and my first major work,* ***In Due Season.*** *The collection of new poems is found in* ***Take My Hand Walk With Me****.*

      The book, In a little corner of a black man's mind stand I..., won an award of recognition from the North Carolina Association of Educators Minority Arts contest in 1997. The poem Autumn's leaves (page 27), the first poem I ever submitted for publication, won 2nd place in Community Pride Magazine's poetry and prose contest in 1996, Charlotte N. C... I really hope that you will enjoy this walk with me through time and change from simple rhythm and verse to more complex thoughts and expressions. I love poetry and want to share that love with you. Enjoy!

Rickey

What people have said about my poetry

"Excellent all-inclusive work Mr. Hood. Words for every walk of life, for every mentality, as only a true poet can do." much respect magi1215

"Great Work....your words are heard as drums.... giving off strength and calls to strengthen.... thanks for sharing!"
2b2b2

"Empowerment of Love 'And I wait, wait patiently for you, for you to turn around, to see you. And I saw your face again, touched by time' Simply Beautiful my Brother Love & Blessings!" "Interesting take on perceptions here brethren... another masterpiece I might add." (from poem, I visited you)
Jellybean22

As you wrote this, so did I close my eyes and joined you in writing poems using the clouds as my blank sheet for the ages! Great write my brother! Peace & Blessings (Poem, Written on High)
HIPJAZZPOET

"I must say I am happy to have found this piece.
First, I must say that the opening line/title is like wicked wild and whoa! Loving it. Blind and near the edge of a pit. Very vivid.

Dancing violently near the edge of the pit. This entire piece is fire. I slipped into oblivion just by reading this piece. May I join you?"
(from, Ignorance is bliss)
Felicia3

"I co-sign to what everyone here had to say. The beauty of this piece is ... you have delivered a whole topic about how we live our lives with only a few words that hit like a hammer."

Book review

This book review is for my chapbook: **Tempest, a collection of poems from an enlightened Nubian soul** *that I published in 1997. This book shows my early works in poetry and taught me the ups and downs of self-publishing.*

From the magazine: Independence Boulevard, October 1999
Published in Charlotte, NC

Poetry Reviews, by Barbara K. Lawing
Tempest: Rickey K. Hood
1997, UniqueVerses Publishing
Does your horoscope ever predict some obscure nothing, and right after you read it, the dumb thing happens? I'd been saying something was true, the astrologer said, but I was advised to check my information to make sure it wasn't erroneous. Soon afterward I began reading Rickey K. Hood's chapbook called Tempest. I didn't like it. The dislike was based on the back cover, where quite a few

editing errors jumped out at me. I very much dislike editing errors. They steal the pleasure of reading. How can I relax and enjoy reading with errors popping up like spooks in a haunted house? They make me want to shriek. But I'd agreed to do the review, so I read on. The music of Hood's lines began to play in my veins. I could hear the rise and fall of his voice as clearly as though he were standing in front of me.

Zing, zing! Zap! He had me. I was enchanted by his musical words. They convey his vitality and joy. After reading this little chapbook, I'm convinced he has the heart of a true poet, marked by a spirit of tolerance –of love for life and the mystery of creation.

Real. That's what his poems are. The rhythms and heartaches and praises and humor unique to African-Americans.

Well, now, I guess is have to admit that horoscope was right. I've been saying poorly edited writing isn't worth reading, Truth is, Hood's book is edited fairly well, but the errors on the cover made me think I wouldn't like it before I ever opened it.

Now don't expect me to read books that are pocked with so many mistakes they look like my legs when mosquitoes work them over, but with that surprising discovery of how much I liked Hood' chapbook, I did some thinking about this poetry revolution we're in the middle of, and decided we must not categorically diss what is poorly edited. In the new world of computer publishing where everybody and his cousin can publish a book, we will cheat ourselves of umpteen grassroots treasures of we confine ourselves to the perfectly edited.

And I do consider Hood's book a treasure. The volume is weak in metaphor though, so I'm hoping in the future he gives due attention to a component of poetry that's just as important as the music: metaphorical imagery.

Fish Out of Water, Ronald M.
1999, Juniper press
The delight of Hood's words coupled with this big change in attitude seemed enough for one day, but there was still a chapbook in the review box: fish out of water. Right away the book gave me the sense that it's full of well-edited and carefully crafted poems. Was my first impressing correct? Yes, but--- with the pleasure of Hood's poems still fresh in my memory, Ronald M. poems suffered by comparison.

Books: Table of contents:

Intro-poem
Take my hand, walk with me

Take my hand and walk with me

Together, let us create

The pages that move us

Through our life's story

Living in our Now

We plant the tree that will

Grow leaves of memory

Leaves blown away by

The winds of time, creating our past

Walk with me

As my partner, taking a journey

On the narrow way up life's mountain

Rough and wonderful

This mountain we must all climb.

Let us write the pages

Plant the tree

Journey up the mountain, together

Come, take my hand, and walk with me.

1995

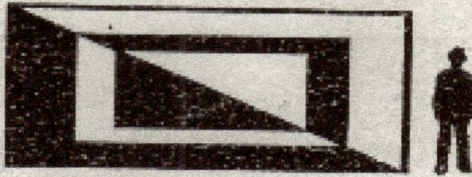

In a little corner of a Black Man's mind stand I...

A collection of poems from the everyday black man

By. Rickey K. Hood

In a Little corner of a
Black Man's Mind Stand I…
(Some poems updated for today)

In a Little Corner of My Mind

Deep in a hidden place of my mind
A little child resides
Alone and fatherless
Lost in a world that's dark and cries

Little boy afraid to live
Afraid to die
Dwells in a little corner of my mind

"Cry baby, cry"
Mama's goin' wipe those tears away
As always
You fatherless child
Come rock in Mama's arms
Grow to be a man
I'll take care of you
As always
You fatherless boy

In the world
A child in a man's mind
Don't know how to live
Just waitin' to die

Cry baby, cry

You fatherless child

Deep in a little corner of my mind

Incomprehensible Concepts

Incomprehensible concepts
Develop for the docile mind
Ask questions, seek answers
Knock over ancient beliefs
To see what you can find

Popular men of enduring fame
They're called God's chosen
Saints/ Prophets/ Messengers/ God incarnate
Whatever!
We line them up to our likes or dislikes
And to them we pledge our
Endeavor

We must take from them their concepts of God
Living according to their truths
As they see it
Or be threatened with damnation
Living in fear of hellish whips
Because of the way another may see it

A loving God who tortures His worshipers
Is a contradiction to me?
A Merciful God who shows no mercy

Is a curiosity to see?

There must be more to the message sent

To make sense of these

Incomprehensible concepts

Ain't No Angel

Here I am with my crooked halo
Dancin' a jig
To some red hot blues

Got crooked wings
Couldn't fly straight if I wanted to
But can shake my tail to some real cool tunes

He's flying high in the sky
On a wing an a prayer
Deacon Righteous got a sweet thang
Playin' truth or dare

Holy sweet thangs, young, tender
Like pretty babies born again
Shouts, "Hallelujah," with lover's passion
As the Preacher moans "Amen"

A lover with a Halo
Cocked to the side
Whether Deacon, Preacher, or little ole me
With sexy crooked wings
There's no place to hide

Frustration

Scream!
As the people walk by

At the top of my voice
I Scream!

The people go to and fro
They look at me in passive curiosity
"Maybe he has something to say?"

I Scream!
As the soft voice flows
My throat tightens as the frustration grows

"Can't anyone hear me!"
"Can't anyone hear me!"

The soft whispers flow in hidden frustration
As – I—Scream!!

That's Life

I work hard for what little respect I get

Serving that damn slave driver makes me sick

But if I'm gonna keep what little I've got

I gotta keep kissing that ass or else they'll know

How much I despise that shittin ass fart

"Go here!"

"Go there!"

"Get this!"

"Get that!"

"Do what I tell you!"

"I didn't give you permission!"

Life's a Bitch, a white Bitch

With dyed red hair

And a silly grin

Out of Control

        I'm in a circle

                I'm spinning catch me

    Help me!

I'm in a circle

                    Spinning and spinning

               And spinning

      I can't stop

                   Take my hand!

    Take my hand!

          Help me!

                 Say what?

       You're in a circle too

Help!

        I'm spinning

            Round… and round I go

      Spinning all around me

              I see

CIRCLES

Tight Rope

Dancing on a wire
With no one around
Far from the heavens
Not far from the ground

Dancing on a wire
High on the town
Afraid if I stop
I may come tumbling down

Pitted

I feel like a pit is in my stomach
A big black hole
I need something… anything
Need to plug it up… fill it up

Come here you fine sweet thang
I ain't got nothin tah give yah
You give it to me
Plug this hole
I'm empty

Is it a pit in my soul… a bottomless pit?
I'll be goin to
Church, Mosque, Synagogue, Temples today
I'll get the spirit… get something
Plug this hole

Masquerade
Trick or treat
Queer of the day
Vacant empty shadows
Am I real?

What's my name?

24

"??"

Trick or treat… masquerade…"OOPS"
My mask fell off

Come on… please
Fill me up
Plug this hole
Can't you understand?
I'm the starved shadow of every man

I'm empty

Reflection

I'm tired of living my life like you
Always with my reflection
Being two

Want to be me… whoever that may be?
Rockin and rollin… flying high in the hay
Riden the wild pony… stroken that pole

Want to be a man
Be me
Be happy
Whatever that may be?

I've been laughing and crying in front of a mirror
Looking at you
At two
Damned tired of wearing this mask
Aren't you?

Walk with me spit in two
Looking behind me
I find me
Watching you

I'm a shadow

Dark on the ground attached to the feet

I only leave when I'm in the darkness

Not when I walk in the light so sweet

Man I'm tired of living

My life for you

Always with my reflection

Being you

Looked in the mirror today

Got tired of looking at an image

Tired of being you

Being two

Need to know how to put myself together

Do you?

Autumn's Leaves

Brazen skin of autumn's hue
Burnt by time/ moistened by dew
Laboring hot/ singing spirituals sway
Raisin head slaves docked at the bay
Planted deep in soil of toil
Seedlings sprout as life uncoil
Strengthened by tears of autumn's rain
Harvest of grapes plump with pain

Pressed against white washed stone
Ooze liquid of life with crimson tone
Offering cups of sacrificed foes
The communion wine/ blood overflows
More are thrown on fields of thorns
Hot sun beat upon them till weary/ worn

My skin is dark like winter's night
Black African/ Son of Kings
Black American/ son of slaves
Who with songs of spiritual sway
Cry tears of moist dew/ day by day

Their beds lie among rotted leaves
Nurturing their children of sundry hue

Upon this soil of hardship and toil

In the land of Autumn

Lies the fallen leaves of

Mother Africa

The Dream

Where have the heroes gone?

The visionaries/ the dreamers?

The black power people?

Fallen/ broken to pieces/ the people

X-- The unknown

The generation without a cause

Generation X/ the undefined people

Fragmented generation/people asleep in the dream

Men and women who marched with King

Their grandchildren have it good

Education, cars, homes, children of their own

Teaching their children how not to be killed by Police

Black churches/ proud to have hosted

The civil rights leaders of the past

Grin and smile as they host President Trump

And we have him only because Black people refusing to vote

After our ancestors give their lives for that right

"Say it loud, black and I'm proud!" but of what?

Seeking equality in all things selfish

Sniffing after material things

Men acting like boys wanting only to father children

He had a dream

Now look at it... at what we've become

A worldwide joke and stereotype

God help us

We lost our way

We need to wake up

Get out of this nightmare

This American Dream

The Projects

Broken glass in street gutters
Wine bottles smashed for fun
Grown men standing on street corner
Joking, tellin stories
Enjoying the sun

Dandelions, roses, daises
Wild flowers growing in uncollected trash
Hides a rat from a stalking cat
With claws ready to slash

Women wearing house coats and slippers
Converse on cement porches
Taking a break from their morning shows
While the rent office men
Fumigate for roaches

Young men skipping school
Looking for some fun
Come across another gang
Looking to draw their gun

Happy laughter is heard about
As children run and play

While dope dealers do their business
With stopping cars/ stopping/ all day

The sky so blue
The grass so green
Life is everywhere
Bird singing, squirrel running
As weapons fire fill the air......POW-POW-POW!!!

Dreams

Dreams/ a bright glimmer of a life/ forgotten

Hopes/ aspirations/ dashed

Forgotten

Little man/ once envisioned big

Fantasized a world where he stood important

A fantasy/ now misplaced

Forgotten

Working for a check to pay a bill and the rent

Life is a check/ to pay bills and rent

Reality is hard/ a dreary drag

A stone on which dreams are dashed/ and

Forgotten

Black

Black! In a land of darkness
Lost in a land of lies
Raping
Stealing
Killing
Gettin yours
Gettin ours
Getting mine
Riding in expensive cars
Hand cuffed
TV/ movies/ speaking lies
Black in a land of ignorance

Black!
In a land of darkness
At home in a world of lies
Always ignoring the truth
Of the working man the woman
The grandparents… the true ties that bind

Those who built this nation
On wounded worn out backs
Now despised by the powers that be

The visionaries who

Planned

Plotted

Strove… and

Died

It's time to arise a young backbone of people

To keep our hopes alive

Black! Behind a darkened veil

Black! In an land on lies

Consumer

I want to buy a brand-new car, a red sporty one
With tinted windows and polished chrome
Loaded with a state of the art
High range transmitting cell phone

I need to buy some brand new clothes
The ones I got last week are old

I gonna buy a new big screen TV
That 25 inch is too small for me

I have to find a new place to eat
 Hungary for…
More things $
        More things $$
                More Things $$$
                        O how sweet

I got best friends who are generous, you see
Visa
Master Card
American Express
Discovery, and more…
They give me what I want, just like it's free

I want it…

I need it…

I got to have it…

And I got it…   The Bill...$$$$$$$$!

Advice

Whenever I want to tell you something

You never have time to sit and listen

Always got some place to go

Runnin' around with those so called friends

Ain't gonna teach you nothin'

Now, sit still boy

Cause I'm not gonna be here forever

And I want you to know something

Before I die…

To Love

1. Here's to Love
   To indifference
   To lust/ to hurt
   To pain/ to pleasure
   To love
   Here's to love
   …again
2. A man who is only a man… (O how common)
   Seeking to have love
   At his side
   Or a prostitute
   Either one will do.
3. Love for mother
   Love for father
   Love for brother
   Love for sister
   Love for God
   If only I could have a
   Love for you…
   Wherever you are?
   Whomever you may be?

   Enough of love
   Now let me rest.

Another love poem

Sailing on a timeless sea
Adrift in your arms
An endless expanse of joy for me
That's how it is to be with you
To be near you/ to hold you
To touch you/ to love you

I love you

1997

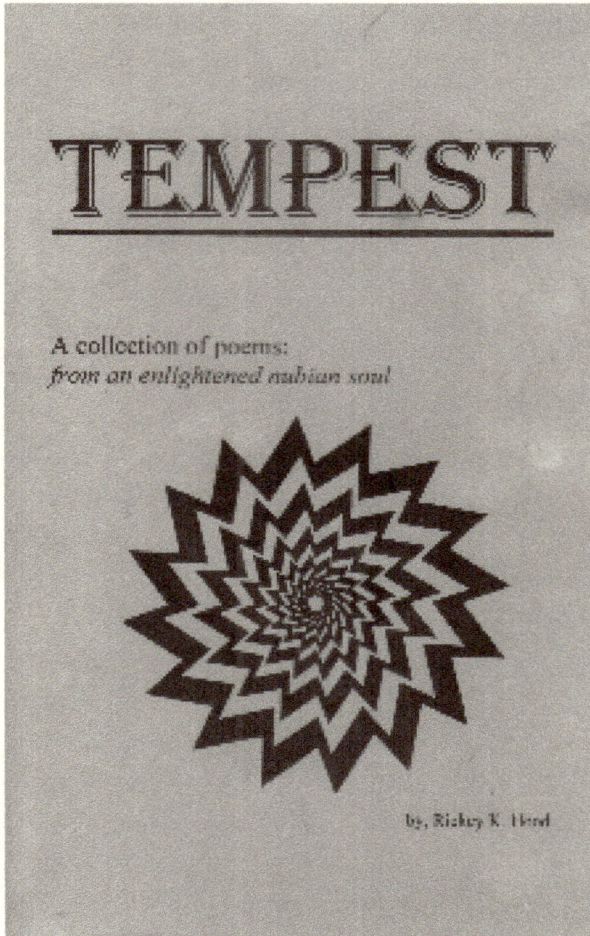

Tempest

A collection of poems

From an enlightened Nubian soul

(Some poems updated for today)

Tempest

The sky above me was thick
Someone had knocked over an inkwell
Dying the clouds black
Ocean swells were high as towers
In the horizon/ lightning set the atmosphere ablaze

Surface beneath me dance a pagan dance
Faster/ and faster/ and faster/ I can't keep up!
A tempest ensued
As the sky emptied thick black drops
Pouring down on my little boat
Adrift in the mist
Blown about by tantrums of the gods

Then/ I saw him/ strolling by
Walking the waves
Like a Californian native
I yelled out to him/ but the storm carried my words away
Then/ he noticed me
Looking at me/ smiling
And said… / Nothing
No/ "peace"
No/ "be still"/… Nothing!

My little boat was sucked into a funnel

I was embraced by sweat and dread

A soaped-up engine pounded in my chest

And just before the frantic banging caused my heart to stop…

I woke up.

The Poet

I'm not here to entertain
You've been entertained
Enough!
I'm here to shake you up,
Make you worry, make you think
Make you work
If you want the truth
Open
Your eyes
Open
Your ears
Open
Your mind
Experience
The poet
It's a message
To the blackman
A message to the whiteman
It's a message to the yellowman
A message to the brownman
It's a message to the gayman
A message to the strightman
It's a message for all my sisters

Listen

To the poet

I speak the truth

I create conflict

I provoke insight

Incite revolution,

Ask… Mazen Maarouf*

The poet

Opens doors to dark house

Turns on every light

So all may see

Pretty pictures/ hung crooked

Hand-made rugs/ on un-swept floors

Polished bathrooms/ with stains in toilets

Trash. Trash. Trash.

Sing. Sing. Sing.

America the beautiful

The poet sees

You haven't washed

The bodies of Native-Americans

Still stick to your feet

Blood of African-Americans

Drip from your whips

Sing.

    Sing.

       Sing.

America the free

The smile on your faces

Comfort not/…one right

Is equal to another

For black folks/ poor white folks

For brown folks/ justice is

$$Expensive$$

        Sing.

    Sing.

Sing.

For American civil rights/ for her human rights

Duplicitous

Like the grins

On her two faces… ask the family victims

Of stand your ground laws and killer cops.

Sing. Sing. Sing.

America the beautiful

Beautiful America

To you

I sing

Hear the words of the poet

I'm not here to entertain

You've been entertained

Enough!!!!!!!!!!!!!!

*Mazen Maarouf: Palestinian poet Mazen Maarouf was raised in Lebanon and recently forced into a double exile in Iceland after criticizing the Syrian regime.

My Dream

This is my dream
To see swords made into plowshares
To see the lion lie down with the lamb
To see drug dealers weeping
For the lives they have taken
To see their customers ask forgiveness
For the life they have wasted

To live in the inner city
With no sound of police
Domestic violence
Cries of a neglected child
To see playgrounds clean
And filled with children at play
To walk the streets
With no fear of stray bullets
To see hand guns melted down
To create life affirming art

This is my dream
That blackmen/ blackwomen
Love one another
More than cars
More than houses

More than jewelry

More than jobs

More than social positions

More than money

That black people

Live in peace and love

As the lion shall do with the lamb

This is my dream

Mothers of the Revolution

For, Nikki Giovanni & Sonia Sanchez

I've been reading Nikki and Sonia

Black poets/ black sisters

Black mothers of the revolution

I been impregnated by

Words

Their words/ growing inside me

Kicking me

Pressing to get out

Of me

I've been reading Nikki and Sonia

Strong black women

Don't take no shit

Black women

Tell it like it is

Bold/ black women

I've been taught

I am

A beautiful black man

I am

A strong black man

I am

A true black man

I am

Pregnant with myself

I am

Giving birth to myself

I am

To be/come myself (the delivery was difficult)

I've been taught

To find my own voice

To shout against silence

To write against the wrongs

To be/ a poet

I've been reading Nikki and Sonia

Black poets/ black sisters

Black mothers/ of the revolution

For, Betty Shabazz

Died June 24, 1997

Down/ down the setting sun

West to dreams

The setting sun

Down/ down the waning moon

North/ to sleep

The waning moon

Sun/   moon

Light/   truth

Husband/ wife

Malcolm/ Betty

Gone   Gone

The setting sun

Gone   Gone

The waning moon

 Down   Down

To sleep

            And dream

An Angry Poem

For Betty Shabazz

He took a match and gasoline

And burned up a grandmother of the revolution

A twelve-year-old grandson of the X

Took a match

And showed just how fucked up

Our children are

He didn't mean to kill his grandmother

He just wanted to warn her

How messed up

Can you get?

He took our grandmother

And treated her like trash/ Took a match

And lit her up

He said, *"I didn't mean to hurt her"*

My young brother,

What's a match

And gasoline

For?!?!

Memories of Sand

We once loved each other

As sand in hand escapes through fingers
Your love, your memory
Empties through fissures
In my soul

A grasp of dry sand
Slipping hastily from my hand
As the sensation of you in my arms
Holding you tight
Shielding you from harm
A closeness too tight… I now see
You slipped away/ where you can breathe
I waited for you

But you…ebbed steadily away as
A night's dream/ once awakened
A love undying/ discovered mistaken
Gone
As sand in my heart
Emptying through cracks
In my soul from the start

A timeless sea of emptying sand

An hourglass
For eternity
This place that is now left for me
A desert for love
And fidelity

Love unrequited
In this place it must rain
To bud forth
A new love
And love obtain

Lost Souls

I know of a young man
Whose eyes are bright/ shinning
Glistening with dead innocence
Skin dark as indigo
Mind keen/ aware
Frustrated/ in his soul
With lust/ for his mother's boyfriends
Them like him too
A father/ what's that?
Scenes in this head/ just doesn't cease
Of a fondle/ here and there
Pushed to the side/ ignored
That's what men do/ he believes
He's only twelve

I know of a young girl
Who speaks of gun shots
Outside he bedroom window
Of her mother's boyfriends (none her father) beating her
With the belt loosened from his waist
Pants fallen to his ankles/ undone/ whispering sweet threats
"I'll kill you if you tell a soul"
Hopes of a beautiful wedding day/ a loving husband
A life/ scratched away by the claws of a cock

"Mama knows/ she has to"

Long braided hair/ frame her brown hollowed eyes

Eyes which have seen too much/ old eyes in a young frame

She's only ten

Lamentations

I'm blind
My eyes are shut tight
I'll no longer see the atrocities
They are squeezed tight
As tears find their way between the lids
Wetting my face
Like the visions carved in my soul

I see them
Eyes! Eyes wide open
Full of fear/ helplessness/ death

The sight of another young black man
Lying dead
Shot down on the streets
A bullet between the eyes
He lie there staring… at nothing
Eyes/ wide open

I'm blind
I will no longer see

I'm deaf
My fingers are in my ears

I will not hear the screams
My fingers are jammed tight
While wailing howls echo through the streets

A mother's lament
Is sung through the city
As she follow behind screaming sirens
Chanting the lyrics "My son, my son!"
Ears stuffed with prayers
That can no longer hear

I'm deaf
I will no longer hear

I'm mute
I can no longer speak
My voice is worn out
From wails and howls
From laments and prayers
From screams and yells

I can no longer say, "Be careful"
I can no longer say, "I'm bailing you out for the last time!"
I can longer say, "Good morning"
Because,

You Are Dead

"My son, my son!"

I can no longer speak
My voice is worn out from grief

It Ain't Nothin' But A Party

dance, dance, dance my big feet
twirl, twirl, twirl my big hips
pay them folks no attention
give'em a reason tah stare

dance, dance, dance my big feet
twirl, twirl, twirl my big hips
shake and shimmy all night long
and give them girls reason tah talk

it ain't nothin' but a party

A Negro Spiritual

For the 21 century

Problems in mah soul

Troubles in mah soul

O' Lawd

O' Lawd

What I'm gonna do?

Gun shot rage

Gun shots roar

Death's gotta uzzie knokin' at mah doo'

Problems in mah soul

Troubles in mah soul

O' Lawd

O' Lawd

What I'm gonna do?

Food stamps come

Doallar bills go

Mama's got thah rent flyin' up her nose

Problems in mah soul

Troubles in mah soul

O' Lawd

O'Lawd
What I'm gonna do?

God on dah shelf
Preachers made tah order
Poppa's gotta 40 getting high on dah corner

Trimblin' in mah soul
Woes in mah soul
O'Lawd, O'Lawd, I'm lookin' fah you

I'm only what you made me!

I'm only what you made me!
You tell me to get back
To get the hell out of your lives
That I make you look bad
I don't know why you'd say that
I'm only what you made me

You tell me to get a job
To get a life
That I make your taxes too high
I don't know why?
I'm only what you made me

Black
(Not in color, but in mind)
A mind full of servitude to you
The man
The white man
(Not in color, but in mind)

Black
In knowledge
A heritage still hidden from me
No light to shine down on this

Black soul
No equality to command
No equality to demand
(Not in color, but in mind)

At his feet
The world has prostrated
Beside me
I see all the peoples of the earth
Red, brown, yellow, black
All bowing before the man
The one that looks like Jesus

He has conquered the world
With missionaries
And televangelist lies
Words reaching out
Putting the world
Under
Its spell
Putting the world to sleep

We sleep
In prostration
To the man
The one that

Looks like Jesus
That white man

Sometimes
I lift my head up

Sometimes
I speak out against injustice and lies

Sometimes
A glimmer of light shines on me

At that moment
I'm no longer black
At that moment
I become
The color of mahogany
The color of oak
The color of cherry wood
The color of pine
Then..
I'm given a sip of wine
A fifth of liquor
A rock of crack
A 40oz of Bull
And told…

"we hear you, we understand your pain"

With a pat on the head
I'm loved back into my place
The moment is gone

I'm **black** again!

Gossip

I am

Invisible/ stealthy/ unnoticed

Moving/ without sound/ speaking/ with soft voice

Touching/ with cold sensation

I am

Standing among you/ working with you

Dinning at your table/ eating your whispers

 CoooooL/ Whissspeeeerrrss

About the defenseless innocent

I am

Your idol/ chit-chat

"What's the buzz?"

"What's the buzzzzzz"

About whom/ I care nothing

I am...

Family Tree

A family tree has lost some leaves
The chill of winter's breath has carried them away
Yet their strong/ soft voices
Continue to resonate through the seasons

Brothers/ sisters I have known
Though never met
They are here with me
Together our stories are chanted
My spirit remembers fresh as the day first told

Of life across time and sea
Dancing to beats of drums
With companions running and playing
Hunting together to kill the wild bore
In struggle/ fighting the men of the great ships
Seeking to set captive souls free
From chains that bound souls

Strapped in the pit of crossing
Praying to see another day
Put on auction blocks
Laboring in fields/ in quarries
                    Building

       Building

Building

Monuments for the generations to come

Nate

      Harriet

           Frederick

               Sojourner

                    Booker T.

                    W.E. B.

              Marcus

          Elijah

        Malcolm

    Martin Jr

Barrack

Seedlings blown and planted across the ages

To land and grow on a distant shore

Strong monuments through the seasons

A foundation firmly rooted

Pushing upward against the cold... My family tree

Blacklash

Sorry, no more race based employment
Sorry, no more race based representation
Sorry, no more race based education

"You mean...
I must be without color to get ahead?"

Yes!
You're just too black

Dedicated to black republicans

Black men reduced to creatures to be studied

My complements to PBS

Anthropologist in the bush/ watching me
Studying me/ a man/ black
Observing me on my job/ in my home
Cooking/ cleaning/ eating
Learning my language/ my life
The greed/ the killing/ the love
He studies me

Data collected
Evidence mounts
Disappointingly revealing
A human being/ a man/ like himself

Argument

One says,
"God has spoken to us
We have his Torah!"

"No!" another says,
"God has spoken to us
We have his Qur'an!'

Still another says,
"God has spoken to us
We have his Gospels!"

I wonder what God has to say?

Writing about New Hampshire

I could write about my home in New Hampshire
About the bubbling brook
That flows peacefully beside the barn
Where the horses drink quietly
After running across the lush meadow

I could write about my father
Who sits on the porch chewing tobacco
Spitting over the front rails
My mother/ who lovingly comes out of the house
Carrying a pitcher of ice cold lemonade

I could write about the times
I sat down with my folks
On the front porch/ laughing/ singing
Enjoying this beautiful scene
On a warm summer's day in New Hampshire

I could write about this…

If I hadn't lived in the projects of Charlotte, NC
Looking out
Over uncollected trash
Pushed to the side of street gutters

Outside my government owned apartment window

My mother
Who raised me
And six other siblings alone
No father to be seen
No child support to be had

I could write about New Hampshire

If not for the hopeless men
Walking up and down neighborhood streets
Selling drugs or some other "hot goods"
Trying to get rid of it fast
Before the police bust'em

I could write about New Hampshire
About my life there…

But/ it would be a lie

U.S.S. Henrietta Marie

A slave ship speaks

A conduit/ a vessel/ a womb full of life I was
I've borne forth children both great and small
In the bow of my hull/ I was pregnant
My stomach ached of chains and swill
Crammed with cries of bitter tears
Prayers to a god/ I know not which
Pain/ birth pains of a people
A great people to be
They were within me

I conceived on a dark ancient shore
I saw them Raped! Violate! Stolen!
Against their will/ I conceived a nation
And brought them to the new world
But many had been slain
Put to death/ by men who violate/ mock
The pain of a people
Dangling like ornaments on a tree
I wept for those within me

As best I could/ I carried my children
I heard their cries/ within me
Chained people/ kicked/ screamed

Yarned to sing/ to dance/ to play the drums

To come out/ see the sky

To be with loved ones/ under the sun

To see the rolling hills/ the wild plains

To run/ to run once more

To be free

But…

They lie there stacked/ cargo/ within me

Side to side/ shoulder to shoulder

Head to foot/ foot to foot

Knee to head/ head to side

Foot to side/ side to knee

I could do nothing but carry them along

On the vast emptiness of the sea

Docking on an alien shore

To give birth to an oppressed people

The ones yearning to be free

The great people to be

They were within me

Time flies

Time
Tic/ tic/ tics
Its slow meticulous echoes
Chip/ chip/ chips away
At little pieces of my sanity

Time
Tic/ tic/ tics
While fingers
Tap/ tap/ tap away
Unconsciously
On the ever patient table
Anxiously
Waiting relief from the
Torturing echoes of that damn clock

"Tic/ tic/ tic/ tic/tic/tic…"
And only a minute has passed

Struggle

With a smile, we said
"Yes sur!"
As we fought your wars
Killed your enemies
Did as we were told
Became your Negro
And when you were done with us
We still equaled
…Nothing

With a smile, we said
"Yes sur!"
As we worked your factories
Sweated in your fields
Cooked and cleaned for your babies
Became your entertainment
Till you became bored
Our usefulness gone
We still equaled
…Nothing

My back/ a plowing mule
My arms/ hammered steal
My mind/ a secret place for plotting

My spirit/ a place of refuge

With a smile
"Yes sur, boss man!"
To messa Europe

With a smile
"Yes sur, boss!"
To messa America

With a smile
"Yes sur!"
To the enslavers of Africans

Dark brother
Truly
Brothers after all
Struggle on

"yes sur! Whatever you say"
WE ARE AFRICANS!

"yes sur, boss Man! Whatever you say"
STRUGGLE ON!

Children of sorrow

Dark brothers
Truly
Brothers after all
STRUGGLE ON!

Yes sir, boss! Whatever you say!
STRUGGLE ON
STRUGGLE ON
STRUGGLE ON
STRUGGLE ON
STRUGGLE ON
STRUGGLE ON
STRUGGLE ON

The Struggle Continues

In our souls
We bear the marks that have not healed
In our hearts
The flame that none can conceal
Wearing the chains of bondage
Enslaved minds and beating wills
As the struggle continues on

Working jobs for little pay
Saying, "yes sur, yes sur"
All through the day
Then come home
Fall on our knees and pray
As the struggle continues on

Eyes full of life shining strong
Voices crying out for justice
Across the White House lawn
Dark flesh bearing the wounds
Of society's wrongs
As the struggle continues on
As the struggle continues on…
Continues on…   Continues on…   Continues on…

Stones

Stones

Rough/ sharp/ from quarries deep

Black/ cool/ on slopes steep

With diamonds/ gems/ emeralds/ rubies

Smooth polished/ like privileged babies

Stones of beauty/ shiny/ hard

Rough/ sharp at its start

Words

Like stones/ how similar they be

To hurt/ maim/ kill

Beautifully

Sweet Dreams

Last night/ I dreamed I was asleep
And while I slept/ I dreamed
I was asleep/ dreaming
About that night
I dreamed
Of you

Small town girl

To the west she saw the setting sun
Silhouettes of pigeons perch on power cords
Fumes of toxic gases rising from factory stacks
Creating the kaleidoscope of a beautiful sunset

She saw streetlights reflecting on freshly rained streets
Acid rain eating away a stone mason towers
Street natives/ dress in tribal artier
Strutting up and down wet city corners in colorful array

The view of the skyline fill her widows
From every window colors of stone
Down below/ mechanized drones
Of steel move alongside fleshly hordes

In the distance/ a setting sun celebrate
The close of another day/ reflecting the colors of a toxic sky
And she whom I took on this mundane tour
Replied/ wide eyed "how lovely/ Oh how lovely"

Problems

Good shotta licker
Take care dah problem
Don't wanna think
Or care tah solve'm

Jus wanna look
In dis silky haze
Float on dah flow
Inna stupor daze

Feelin' comin up
Gotta earl, gotta go
Clean myself en
Mop dah floo'

Club scenes nice
If ya gat problems
Good shotta licker
Help ya solve'em

Party

Putta nickel in dah piccolo

Picka tune

Do a litty diddy shuffle, baby

Make her swoon

It nothin' but a party, move

Make some room

Cuttin' dis rug up, honey

Gi-me a broom

Nothin' but a party, girl

Drink it up

Says y'alls glass empty, sugar

Take my cup

Life'sah playin' on a piccolo

Pick a tune

Nothin' but a party, yah!

Give me room

(Piccolo, old word for Jukebox)

2000

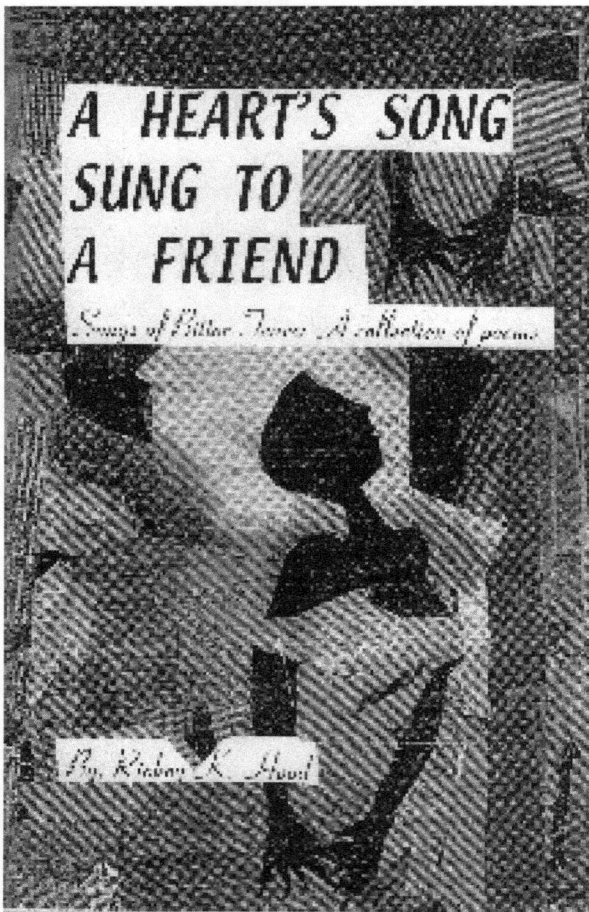

A Heart's Song Sung to a friend:

Songs of bitter tears

(Some poems updated for today)

Can I help?

A child is crying

With a skinned knee

His mother raising him alone

To become a man

Putting on his first prison numbers

To have sons

Running the streets wild with no man at home

To be a laborer

Working hard toward an early grave

To have daughters

Looking forward to being a single mother and on warfare

To be a drug dealer

Selling death to children on the streets

To watch our babies

Kill each other because they haven't learned to care

To become Soldiers

Of the ivory tower

Answering the master's call

To Kill/ Kill/ Kill

With war/ torture/ rape

All in the name of capitalism/ oil/ God

To Kill

With words/ bullets/ grenades

To Kill/ Kill Kill

While a child is crying
With a skinned knee
Waiting for someone to say
"Can I help?"

Capitalism

I am created for you
A culture that worships the dollar

I am created by you… POW!   POW!
Give me your pocketbook bitch!

Holy Performers

With bulging eyes and mouth opened wide
(Bringing images of a fish gasping for breath)
The Preacher!
Thunders/ his baritone voice
Captivating his audience

Stage lights shine/ giving that heavenly glow
Makeup covering every spot and blemish
(Perfect/ perfect let the video cameras roll)
With snarls/ grunts/ shouts
And banging of fist he reaches up
To bring heaven down

Jerks and convolutions
Ripple through the aisles
Yells and shouts
For mercy, "Lord have mercy"
Echo across the pews
As white-gloved matrons
Usher to fan the flame into a frenzy
As… Holy Spirit flies everywhere
The Word of God slaying
Without respect
Of persons

The preacher

Has God in his coat pocket

Every once in awhile

He brings Him out

Quotes a verse or two about hell

Look pleased with himself

Then puts Him back

His audience is pleased

Every Sunday they return/ early

To sit eagerly waiting

For his show to begin

Spring Afternoon

Bright/ intense sun wash
The landscape/ peeling back
Layers of hue
Embedded in the foliage

A gentle/ soft breeze cools
My face/ as I smile at the sight
Of blue birds/ and red birds
Waltzing in air

Welcomed shadows stretch-out/ of
Tall dogwoods/ maples/ pines
Perfuming the air/ casting
Shade for a late afternoon picnic

To the Beat

Rrrat/ tat/ tat

Move/ rhythms flow

Over my body

Hot/ cool/ spicy

Rhythm hum/

Burn through fleshy

Ear/ drums

Beat/ beat/ beat

Drums of my soul/

Carries away/ by way

Of tribal instinct/ move to

Beat/ beat/ beat/

Of rhythmic/ rhythms moving in

Rrrat/ tat/ tat

Jazzy flows/

Down on my flesh

Excite/ stimulate

Reconnect/ mind/ spirit/ body

To home

Beats

Of Africa

What it is to be Black

Under the pressing press

I strive

Beneath the grinding stone

I thrive

Yet/

By the grace of God

I survive

Song of better tears

(A choreopoem)

I.   Two voices (opening scene)

<u>**Narrator**</u>

Voices of a people

Sing songs of better tears

Tears of want

Tears of lack

Tears for being black in America

Where is he to be?

Where is he to go?

Expect to the street corners

Or public playgrounds

To hang out with the boys

<u>**Man**</u>

Where am I supposed to be?

Where's this black man to go?

To the Million Man March?

I missed it that year

I was busy…

Getting high that day

I was busy…

Smack'en the hell out of my woman that day

I was busy…

Calling her bitch/ whore/ slut that day

I was busy…

Getting drunk that day

If I had remembered

I would have taken that day off

Oh well

Maybe next year

Woman

A smile etched in stone

But at one time in flesh

But that was a long time ago before

Before I got "saved"

Before I got filled

With the illusions of their words

Before I got serious with God

Or… was it God

I was told it was God

I had problems then

Problems

Problems with my man

With my life

I was his wife

I wanted to be a good wife

So
I went to the house
For worship
And I began to clean
Myself up

I was told
"people of faith should always be joyous"
I was told to
"Let go and let God, He'll handle all your problems"
I was told
"God is always right on time"
But
I had problems that wouldn't go away

Was I a woman of
faith?
Or a liar
A liar to myself?
To my man?
To my God?
Now I really had problems
Problems
Problems with my life
My man
My God!

Man

Don't fuck with me!

I'll blow your motherfunkin brains out.

Tah-hell wif all yall educated niggas

I make mo money in an hour than you make in a week

So don't fuck with me

I gat a good thang gonna on

You can buy a hit of it

Or you can just leave me the fuck alone!

Woman

I was told

"submit to your man"

I was told

"submit to your God"

I was told

"Trust in the Lord" and that "everything is gonna be alright.

So, I did

I SMILED *(big fake smile)*

Man

I ain't askin for your damn help!

I didn't ask for your help

You ride around in your white shirts and bicycles

Knocking on my doo waking me up out of my sleep

Try'in to winess to me.

Try'in to tellin me I'm going to Hell

because I don't want to be bothered with your ass

You say…

You want to save my soul?

You say…

You want Jesus to have my soul?

Then tell him to give me a job

A good job

And yah… If he's gonna be livin here

Tell him to help me with the rent

Put food on the table

Buy some nice clothes for my wife and kids

And get these damned drug dealers

Off my doo step

Tell Jesus to do that for me

I'm tired of asking

Woman

I smiled/ a lot *(with a big fake smile)*

I prayed/ a lot!

I put up with that man/ a lot!

I repented/ a lot!

I was told

"be patient"

I was told

"God will work a miracle in His own time"

I was told

"just be patient"

And so… I was

One month

    "BITCH!" *(man)*

Six months

    "SMACK!"

Two years

    "Where the hell you think you're going?" *(man)*

Six years

    "I don't know why I keep you around!" "SMACK!"

Ten years…

        I've

                Been

                        Patient! *(Look of frustration)*

Man

What's wrong with you?

You just don't get it

Leave the bitch!

Let her have the kids

The bills/ the rent

Hang out with us/ the boys

On the corner

We got a 5th of liguor/ I"ll share it with you

All you need to do is pack up

And leave

Don't worry about your family

Welfare will take better care of them

Than you ever could

They'll pay the rent

Put food on their table

And even get them new clothes

All you have to do

Is leave

Think about it/ my brotha

Just think about it.

<u>Woman</u>

That man is still here

Happy with me and my Smile

As I...

Swallow down Prozac

And keep the appointments

For my weekly group sessions

I've been a little depressed

But *(being fake happy)*

"People of faith don't have such problems"

As I have been told

I hope God is pleased

Please/ be pleased

My face is tired

Being etched in stone (*Big fake smile)*

(close scene)

(next scene open)

II.   So, I hear you're faggit

Man 1

So, I hear you're a faggit?

Man 2

I prefer homosexual or gay

Though I've heard it said we're sexually challenged

Man 1

Cute jok

Man 2

No, sad

Man 1

Ever been with a woman?

Man2

Been married

Man1

Yah?

Man2

It was a religious thing.

Thought I'd please God by sacrificing myself

Man1

What happened?

Man2

I got tired of dying daily/ the woman was killing me

I decided I wanted to live

Man1

You still talk to your wife?

Man2

We speak…

(telephone rings, man 2 answers)

Man2

Hello…

Damit! I told you I'll be over at my usual time

Ex-wife

"I got things I need to do this morning

You need to come over here right now and get these chaps

Or you can just forget about pickin'em up this weekend."

Man 2

Look here! Every weekend there's something

You just gotta do. Goddamnit I'm…

Ex-wife

" I said I got things to do this morning,

Now if you're tellin me you don't want to spend time

With your kids this weekend…"

Man2

Dammit! I'm getting real tired of your shit!

Every weekend it's always something.

I told you I'll be there

Ex-wife

" You just want to hang around with your fag friends/ you ain't shit.

And I don't want my children hangin around them either.'

Man2

Bitch/ I'm getting real tired of you!

Ex-wife

"faggit" *(Click)*

Man 2 says to Man 1

Like I said/ we speak

III. Church

Man 1

You said getting married was a religious thing?

Man 2

Yes, I did

Man 1

You must have went to church a lot
Ever tried Jesus?

Man 2

Yah/ I did
I remember waiting for that Born Again experience that the
Hot Gospelling/ Spirit Filled/ Blood Washed/ Blood Bought/
True Children of the True Church of the Living God in Christ
Preachers prophesied would happen after accepting
Jesus as lord and savior.

I fasted/ prayed/ and condemned myself
For the sin of / Being myself.
I had hands laid on me
Supposed demons casted out

Filled with the spirit

And spoke in tongues.

I shouted

I danced

I stumped my feet

And raised my hands

I cried out/ "thank you jesus!" and "jesus save me!!"

All while rushing down

To the alter to receive a word

From the mouth of the preacher

"Remember to give your 10% tithe and your 10% offerings,

And we have books, and CD's on sale in the lobby"

Amen.

Man 1

Sounds like you been through it.

Man 2

Yah I have/ and bein' who I am doesn't make it any easier

But/ I'll make it/ I'll make it.

(Scene close)

(next scene open)

IV. The Blur

Narrator

How sad that one should lose freedom to gain it

A paradox of comic force

A yin/ yang

A light/ darkness

A good/ evil

A woman and her man

A poisoned/ love

Woman

…and I sit, looking out

Through the tangled mesh lining her office window

Looking out over the bobbed wire fence

Framing my life/ trying to remember

The blur of that night.

He was dunk/ again

I was afraid/ as always

As always/ I tried my best to make no mistakes

On those nights so he'd have no excuse/

His fits were unpredictable/ raging/

The kids knew to run into bedroom those nights

They know the routine

(lock the door behind you/ if necessary

Jump out the window and run for help)

He looked relaxed/ lying on the couch

Laughing at some joke in his head

(Go to sleep/ just sleep)

Then he started

To be playful/ rubbing his hands

Up my thigh/ my nightgown/ between my thighs

to foreplay inside me/

I stood there/ giggling/ smiling

Hoping he'd pass out

     But something snapped

He got up from the couch/ wild eyed/ grinning

And jammed his middle finger inside me like a hook

He gabbled my hair/ slammed my face to the floor

Climbed on top of me biting my breast calling me

Bitch/ whore/ slut/ and shouting/ "who else been up in here?!"

He undone his pants and forced himself inside me

It hurt/

     He hurt me bad/ so bad/

          I screamed

My son came out of the room

     (He knew better than to come out of the room!)

"Stop/ hurting mama!!"

     / he tried to help me

"Get off my mama!!"

    / he screamed

But the man he never learned to call father only got angrier

He got off of me/ while beating me in face

He took his fist and punched out three teeth

And fractured my right eyes socket

I don't rember feeling pain/ I don't know why?

My son was still screaming/ trying to help me

But his sometimes father

Slammed his fist into my boy's left temple

He collapsed on the floor/ not moving

Then came the blur

I can't remember much of what happened next

I do remember a shot

Someone holding something/ it could have been a gun

It felt like a gun

My next clear memory

Was when I was surrounded by paramedics

I saw them carry away a body bag

My heart stopped/ "that son-of-bitch killed my son"

Just then I heard his voice/ "it's ok ma/ I'm here"

He was in the ambulance with me

Sitting beside this sister/ she was shaking

He was bruised faced and crying

They held my hand/ hard

              /and I fell asleep

 The next morning

I woke up a window and a murder

My baby girl started having nightmares

Not long after I went away

My son says she can't remember her dreams (or don't want to)

She always wake up wide eyed/

Exited with fright/ crying out for mommy

Sometimes I lie in bed imagining

I'm holding her in my arms

I want so much to be with here/ to let her know it's alright/

She did the right thing

But/ I can't

Today was a good day

Talking to the state psychologist

I just felt like talking

And as usual

She sits in her corner

Taking notes

Strange

How one must lose freedom / to gain it

(last scene open)

V. That Morning

<u>Man</u>

I woke up in jail this morning/ again

I don't mean to hurt my woman

She's all I got

But I get so tired of hearing

All that damn naggin'

Come out her mouth

"you staying out late again!"

"you came home drunk again!"

"you lost your job again!"

"you fucking around on me again/ ain't cha!?"

" You ain't shit!"

Then I said

"Your Mama ain't shit!"

(SMACK!!!)

She smacked me

Tired to gouge out my eyes

She kicked me in the groin

Hit me upside my head with something hard!

She was trying to kill me!

It was then/ only than/ in self defense

I took my fist

And knocked the living shit out of her

She calmed down

Later that night

The police came/ woke me up

Charged me with spousal abuse

And took me way

They didn't want to hear my side of the story

 So/ what am I to do?

Where's this black man to go?

To the Million Man March?

I went

I came home/ atoned/ calling my woman

Nubian queen

Mother earth

Teacher of generations

Wife of god

I lavished her with roses

Kente' cloth dashikis
And she loved me
With her body and soul
Until
The night I came
Home late/ again

That morning
I woke up in jail

(The End)

Brothers

For my brother Ronnie E. Hood (Regene)

Two hands intertwined
A private communion
A strong bond not easily broken
Two in love, two in unity
"He's my brother"

Nurturing and compassionate
A comfort for my weary eyes
Strong ground to steady myself
"He's my brother"

A help in times of trouble
A sturdy fortress is he
A refuge were I my rest from stress
"He is my brother"

2012

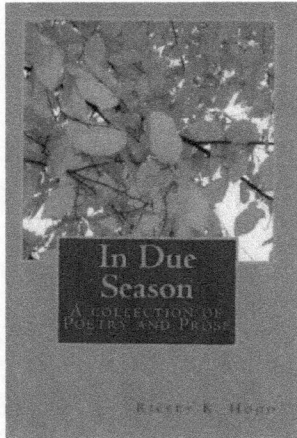

In Due Season

A collection of poetry and prose

Love

...and you spoke to me
With your wide puppy dog eyes
Crying/ playing havoc with my emotions
Screaming words that penetrate
As hot razors/ slashing my heart

As much as I try not to stare
I stare/ into your eyes/ trying to find
The words/ the right words
But finding only echoes of our mutual dislike
Vomiting forth from my mouth

Yet/ somewhere in the flow
I formed the words
I love you

Just the thought of you

It fogs my mind to think of you
My nature rises with the mere thought
I can't help myself
When I remember smoothing my rough hands
Over your smooth form
To be intoxicated with wanting you
Tasting you with my whole self
My senses filled with the rapture of you
Taking in the warm nature of you
To be filled with all of you
Your heat inside of me
Oh, just the thought of you/ fogs my mind

Hide and Seek

I'm hiding from you
In plain sight I'm hiding
The thought of being with you
Is a thought that excites my flesh to blush

To brush my hand
Against yours/ by accident?
Makes me to know the warmth
Of your skin

I wish you could
See me
Hidden before your face
Hoping that one day
You'll think/ to look for me.

Smile

You make me smile
With your sexy charm
I forget myself and sometimes
Move too close/ we're not a couple

But/ you don't pull away/ at less/ not right away
But for a moment
You stand close enough for me to feel your heat

You feel so warm/ not even touching
I can just imagine the day/
That day of us touching/ freely

Touching your warmth against mine
This is fantasy/ I know/ or
Maybe a hope/ a far reaching hope
A "who knows the future" kind of hope
Maybe just a false hope
I just hope/ you feel the same
Seeing that I make you smile too.

What's the Problem?

There's no need to say goodbye…
I heard you say it in your voice the last we spoke
To guess what happened would be just that…a guess?
Because I don't know what happened…what changed for you

I know that I did not change…at less I don't believe I had changed
But time can force changes
It has a way of making things known to the other
That was not known before

That's natural when people meet and get to know each other
But the basic personality, the person
That you said hello to the day we met
Did not change with time

I am still Rickey
And if being me is the problem
I will be me, and
Your problem is with you

No Shame in Love

There is no shame in love
No condemnation/ no law against it
Who can legislate it?
Define its perimeters?
Define the bounties of whom one can love

Love is not observant of constitutional amendments
Love cares nothing for religious debates
The conservative right has no power to control it
The liberal left has no ownership of it

No one created love/ but all are subject to it
Love needs no one's approval…
Marriage license or certificate
To love/ is human
To love/ is divine
Love never fails

No Greater Love

No greater love
Is there between us
That I should love you
So completely
No greater joy
That I should have you
By my side

My life is yours
Take it and live
Let the sweet breath
From my lips kiss you
One last time
Then I will pass quietly
With the taste of
Love on my lips

Oh, what joy it is to be loved
And to love
My life is yours
Take it and live
There's no greater love than this

The Power of Words (5 Proverbs)

A whispered word can be
Carried through the air
As a leaf carried by the wind

Angry men calm their voices
To hear a faint passing word
Their anger cools as they strain to listen

Soft words caress the troubled mind
Tempest thoughts are smoothed so that
A confessed heart can find a direction

A wise man never shouts
His wisdom to the crowd
Rather, he speaks softly his words
To those who want enlightenment

Happiness, like love, is in the eyes
Of the beholder.
And happiness, like love, is often sought
In the arms of illusion

Take My Hand
Walk With Me

Poems from

2013-2018

Freedom #2

Free, freedom!
I see freedom coming my way
Bright shining, bright shining…
Bright shining freedom, freedom is coming my way

I see colors once more
Colors in my world, once gray
Colors in my world… my eyes see colors
In my world again

The door of my future is opening
Opening… opening wide
Opening wide enough for me to step through
To rush through, to run through, to fly through

Free, freedom
I see freedom coming my way

At turning 50

Candles flicker in the dark
Its light casting shadows against
A fading backdrop of
Pastel wallpaper

It's too cool, for this time of year
Too damp. My fingers ache
From the cool dampness
My hair, my eyes, my voice
Fade with time

Time flickers as a candle
Its light dims like faded pestle wallpaper
My bones, cool with age
And the candle's heat
Is not enough
To warm them.

March 10, 2007

I don't have a job right now
I'm worried
But what can worry do
But make my life worse

I come to the park
To sit and write
To feel like nothing's wrong
But I'm still worried/ I can't help it

I see happy people/ families
Walking back and forth pass me
Their dogs stop to sniff me
And it only reminds me of how alone I am

Alone and unemployed
My past/ swept away
My future forming before me/ but not complete
And I'm still worried/ but hope helps

Today

The cool morning air
Breaks over my flesh
Waking my body
Renewing my soul

It is... Today
A day that has never been before
Nor ever come again.
I am born again... Today

For the first time... Today
I see the sun
Feel its heat... made new... Today
I am alive again

Clap your hand and shout
Today is come
Let the spirits of the ancestors shout
Let Africa shout
Let America shout
Let the morning sing

Today is come!
Blessed be the welcome of ...Today!!

Jim Crow In The Holy Land

Talks of peace
Are as leaves of an olive branch dipped in blood
Of generational homes of native people bulldozed
Because they are not of the chosen people

To be citizens in a country
Where you are not wanted
Feared/ because you refuse to be oppressed
Hated/ because they do not ask for what is theirs
Demonized/ for being alive

It was done in America
With the Native-Americans/ African-Americans
Taught to South Africa with the Natives-Africans
Now it comes to you/ with the backing of U. S. funding

Welcome to the Holy Land

White

Waves of cotton
Fan over fields ripe for picking
Bring images of foaming surf
Washing across blenched sands

Blue sk/eyes rest in air
Clothed in drifting robes of clouds
From it the snow falls
That blanket the earth in beautiful pale death

Labor-some/ fair/ and deadly is white

The Wine Makers

The wine makers came to our village today
Dressed and ready to work
I saw as they gathered up the grapes
And readied them for the press

Under foot did they crush the grapes
Painting their boots crimson with the dew
They pressed/ 'till the wine overflowed
And the streets were made drunken
From the flow

And everywhere/ ruby droplet stains marked
The pressing of the wine and the grapes
And the wine makers/ maddened by their drunken frenzy
Cheered as they moved on to the next village

And I/ from my hiding place/ witnessed the horror of it all

You Are Welcomed

Beautiful, there is no other word
No adjective to describe who you are
A kind loving face with a soul to match

Your voice flows over me like living water
From a streaming brook refreshing me with joy
To behold your eyes is to see blazing sun rays
A fire that burns in the limbs

You hold me, not because I am weak
But for the pleasure of being close
And I take comfort in your strength
Your kindness, your patients

How much the pleasure of hearing your laughter
And your voice calling my name
I have dropped my defenses
And opened the door for you to come in
Make yourself at home
To be welcomed

Beautiful

(you are welcome, rewrite)

Beautiful, there is no other word
No other adjective to describe who you are
A kind loving face with a soul of Jasmin

Your voice flows over me like water
From a streaming brook, refreshing, joyous
To behold your eyes is to see blazing sun rays
A fire that burn to the limbs

Tight, you hold me, not because I am weak
But for the pleasure of being close
And I take comfort in your strength
Your kindness, your patients

How much the pleasure of hearing your laughter
And your voice calling my name
I have dropped my defenses
And opened the door for you to come in
Make yourself a home… to be welcomed

I have no words to tell you how I feel\
No words to tell you how you have brighten my life
But to say it is beautiful.

Sweet Deception

Why is love so like tainted wine
So bitter sweet to my lips
Day after day I chase her moody embrace
To find it is as embracing the wind

Unkind and shallow is she
Enticing fools to her breast
Whispering promises she has no intention of keeping
Here kisses are lies
Her touch are fingers of deceit

What can a mortal do?
But bow to her whims
And accept fates curl embrace
To imaging she is kind, warm, caring
And sweet to my lips

Foreplay

Cores hands rub
Against my flesh
With a rough caress
    A working man's hand

Lay those hands against my breast
And kiss them with your thick dark lips
And handle me gently
    With your tongue

Embrace me
While moving your
Hands across my back
Holding me to your working man's chest
Kissing me with those working man's lips

    Making love to me

Man to Man

Why are you staring me down
Like I can read your mind
What do you see?
Someone you want/ to satisfy an urge

I may be willing/ but staring me down
Is not a proposition
Staring me down don't reveal
What's in your head

I'm not the one to inquire about your curiosity
About your DL status
If you're the man/ be the man
And stop being a pussy
Talk to me

Strong Hands

My strong hands in your strong hands
Two strong hands holding each other tight
My body feeling your body
The roughness of your touch
The tenderness of your strength
Your body wanting the smoothness of my body
The heat of my mouth
The firm muscles of my chest
Two strong forms holding each other/ tight
Loving each other

To Notice You

Your voice first caught my attention
A kind of soft low base/ wet with
Sex/y inflections
A thick bodied voice/ full of black
Frustrations/ and hunger
A perfect voice to match your
Thick bodied form

African strength flex's in your arms
Your chest
Your thighs
That ass
Dark black-brown hue covers you
Like layers of Hershey's chocolate
Making all that I see
Catch my attention.

Keeping up Appearances

There is this guy

Don't know him/ but wish I did

Dark skinned man with a full face beard

Eyes full of life and life's pain

Face stern and fearsome as a Mandingo warrior/ till he smiles

And I see just how beautiful he really is

And I smile back/ melting into his gaze

He doesn't know me/ a man like himself

I'm careful to keep that private

But he sometimes sneaks a glance my way on the sly

And watches as I melt/ smiling back

And still/ I keep up appearances

At First Sight

I see you standing there…

Wanting me

Your eyes looking upon me with lust…

Wanting me

To reach down and handle you

Wanting me

To grip you/ stroke you/ tongue you

Wanting me

To explode on you/ in you

Wanting me

To rest my sweaty nakedness beside you

Wanting me

To hold you/ kiss you/ say that I want you

Wanting me

To come over and introduce myself to you.

Chance Meeting

You touched me on my chest
A casual brush against my right nipple
And in that moment I realized…
The moment was gone

No time to savor your fingers
Against my nipple
A phantom caress of memory
Is all that clung to it

A hope of another chance meeting
With those strong hands
Is worth waiting for
To satisfy my imagination

I heard God Laughing

While sitting in the park
I heard the laughter of children
Loud and wonderful
Pouring down as rain on budding leaves
And it was then I understood
That it was God I heard laughing.

The soft still voice of the wind
Broke forth in a belly shaking laugh
Filling the air with a pure unconditional joy
A good belly laugh not filled with wrath,
Vengeance, punishments or judgments

I was surprised to hear that is was
Not a "look at man's foolishness" laugh
Or, God is laughing at us, laugh
But instead, God is laughing with us
Enjoying the joy of the day

Now I can hear the happiness of God
Whose laughter rains down on us
Through the joy of children

Perfect

It's more perfect/ than the first time
I saw your face/ laughing aloud
In the bright sunshine
When your eyes met mine and we both
Blushed/ pretending not to notice
Our first word to each other/ common place/ used too often
But effective... "Hi"

How can it be/ more perfect than the first time
We kissed after our first date/ night stars making
Wishes in our starry-eyed gaze
Us not knowing how or when to say goodnight
And all the night dreaming of us

How can it be
That two would come to share happiness and sadness
Joys and despair/ to be a friend and love to each other
On this day we share our vows/ to become one

It is more perfect/ than the first time
I saw your face/ laughing aloud
In the bright sunshine

Water

Give me water
To ease my thrust
Fresh, cool, life-giving water
Pulled up from the deep well.

Give me water from the cursed ground
The hated ground, the spat on ground
Abused and misused ground
Throw the bucket in there, fill it up

Give me water that rains from on high
Living water that resurrects the earth
That brings forth the harvest
That refreshes the soul

I say again, "Give me water"
That I may bathe and baptize
Splash and play and be renewed
With every drawing from the well

Ground

The ground, the despised ground
The ground that is spat on
Walked over, bury the dead
Shitted on, pissed on
Thought nothing of
Because it's dirt.

The ground
That grow the trees
That create the woods and the forest

The ground that grow the grass
That carpets the land
The ground that brings life to the seeds
That grow the food that feeds the world

The ground over watch sweet waters flow
As rivers and streams
That quench the thirst.

The ground that create the treasures of the heart
The diamonds, gold, silver, sapphires, rubies
And oil the blood of industry.

All these precious things of the despised ground

I am the ground

Plato's Cave Worshipers

Dark sanctuary
Full of shacked worshipers
Sing songs of praise, hear words from the preacher
Shout halleluiah, stand and kneel in prayers
They stare at flickering candles
That creates shadows of religious virtues

Shafts of light slip through cracks
In the door
True light from the true source
But no one notices
They're too busy worshipping
Before flickering candles

I Visited You

It was cold on the night I visited you
The air piercing thick with chill
I moved across the border of your home
And as a silent thief
Did I enter in through the door

With expectations of seeing you
I, as a bird, flew upstairs to the bedroom, but you were not there
Then down again weaving through the halls of the house
To find you, but as I should have known
You were busy in the kitchen

Your back was turned towards me
I know you have no time for conversation
You have work to be done, dinner to cook,
Pots, pans, and cutlery to wash

And I wait
Wait patiently for you
For you to turn around, to see you
And I saw you again, your face touched by time
Aged by life's labors and I smiled
It is beauty, the beauty of your face

And when you looked my way
I saw the color of my eyes seeing you
The smile on my face still loving you
And for a moment
For that fleeting moment of memory
We were together again

Heart

It pains me

Pains me to think you may be gone

It is bothersome to feel that

I'll be alone

Your heart is broken

And you have to get it fixed

Again

Like Sunshine

Death has no grasp on me
Not foot hold or power
As I walk through the valley of shadows
I greet each shade with a smile

I am without time
Giving substance to reality
Nothing can be taken
To the world of shadows/ but me
And nothing can the dead give the living/ but me

I am a joy to the living
A comfort for the dead
I am that which gives meaning
To the eternal circle

Those that stand in my light
Has no fear of the darkness of death
For my love radiates from their graves
Like sunshine

And I shall be with them always
Always, and always….

And you shall know the truth

1.

Truth is like…

The thorns on a rose

The claws on a kitten

The bees around a comb of honey

Those that want the truth

Must also accept the discomfort

The come with it

2.

Knowing what is true

And understanding what is true

Does not bring about

Change in one's life.

Change does not come from the truth

But from embracing the discomfort of truth

Knowing it is part of your healing.

3.

What is truth?

Truth is that which is not a lie.

A lie is that which is passed along,

Three is One and One is three

A man is God and God is a man

And that five pillars of rituals

Can make one pure.

The teaching of a man to men.

4.

Truth cannot be taught as easily as a lie.

Because truth hurts, and challenges complicity

Truth encourages change and demands that you think.

Reason is the teacher of Truth and the dispeller lies.

The Ancestors

For Lavonya

I hear the sound of wind
Laughter pouring forth as a libation
Joyous memories speaking to us
With the voices of the ancestors

The ancestors, our family
Mothers, Fathers, Sisters, Brothers,
Nephews, Nieces', Uncles, Aunts, Cousins
Their memories are now part of telling the family story

We shall all be with the ancestors
That great cloud of witness
Looking down on us, cheering us along in this life.

Our transition will not be the end
We will still be here, in our families love
Keeping memories and the spirit of family alive

A Dark prayer

In shadow/ in halls of blackness
My soul hangers'… Wild!
Out of control
Like a man starving for his last meal
I would eat anything
To stop this pain

I feed/ yet I am never full
My plate overflows
With the meats of
Desire/ want/ loneliness/ lust
All arranged as delicate morsels
Pleasing to the eyes
But every time I dine on these
Pleasures they are without
Flavor/ form/ or substance
Yet every time I hunger
I return to this dinner
Of shadows/

I have worshipped
In churches and found no satisfaction
For my hunger
I have worshipped

In Mosques and found not satisfaction

For my hunger there.

I have worshipped Jesus

And I've followed Mohammad

And found no satisfaction from them

Is my fate in this life

To be nothing more than a plater

Of phantom morals

I am told God is the key

To this hunger/ to unlock

The door and bring light once

Again into the dark heart

To bring color to my soul

And find satisfaction for my wantonness

To still my hunger if I delight in him.

But my God/ I need you to show me

Because I just don't know how

Ignorance is bliss

Let us dance in the night
Beneath a moonless sky
Blind to the world
Near the edge of the pit

Let the music rage
Fill our hearts and souls with passion
As we dance violently
Near the edge of the pit

Echoes call out to us
"Watch your step, watch your step"
Disembodied voices saying nothing worth while
As we dance in time near the edge of the pit

What joy it is to be free
Twirling, twirling in the darkened sky
Free of the cares of the world
Slipping unnoticed into the pit of oblivion

Night Comes

A long day into night
Has overtaken me
Fading rays of the sun
Create kaleidoscope skies
That fade into twilight gray
Not quite night/ not quite day

An in between
Time
Of fading colors
Of fading time/ creeping
More noticed than before

An in between
Time
Not day/ not night
Fading steadily into
The long arms of the dusk

Waiting to see the Dawn

To see you again
Is like waiting to
See the dawn

Shafts of light
Piercing the darkness of night
Driving it back
Like a vanished foe

Arise my love/ stretch-out
Take my hand
Let me see your face
Once again

Let your beauty
Illuminate my world
Causing me to smile

To see you again
Is to relieve my aloneness
As the mornings' dawn
Relives from the pain of night

Written on High

The sky is a sheet to write upon
Leaves of clouds turn as pages
Calling me to write verses
That will fill the horizon like a morning's dawn

From mountain top to valley and plains
My words will blaze the sky
Pages and pages of clouds waiting for me
To scribe my verses

I will reach up and tear down a leaf of sky
And write poems that the mighty ones will read
Angels will love every word
Sharing my verses amongst themselves
But the Fallen ones will scoff in envy

As for man/ only those
Who love the sky
Will see my words
Written on high

Give me the Sky

I wish not to be as the fallen ones
Foolish angels that loved the flesh
And forsook their natural creation
Of winds of mercy

But why can't I be
As a feather on the wind
Raising with ease
On the back of a breeze

To go up, climb up
Higher, higher to live on high
With the breath of the winds
To fly and not fall

Let the ground fall away
Let the world spin and quake
Let the earth and the oceans
Fight amongst themselves…
Just give me the sky

And I shall dress myself in clouds
Bathe in the storms
The four winds will be my consorts

Lightning and thunder my lovers

If only I can forsake my nature of creation
How I wish I was more that dust
More than a mortal
Man of Clay

Gods

I once worshipped a moth
Its powdery white wings
Fluttering in space
Flying in a zig zag dance
In the open air.
And I thought "what a wonderful
Elegant god"
Until the day I saw
The moth god try to land
On a lit torch.
What a sad yet beautiful sight
To see a god incinerate in flames.

Then I worshiped the lit torch
The destroyer of moths
But this god was different
It has too many demands, needing me
To attend its needs like a parent to a child.
Needing to be fed constantly to keep its flames alive.
But one day as I was feeding the torch it began to rain.
I could do nothing to keep the flame alive,
The water was killing it, till it died.

Enlightenment

Enlightenment is not something that just happens in an epiphany
Daily meditation or quite contemplation
Nor can it be found in dogma, strict codes of living life,
Religion or discovering the meaning of ones supposed existence

Enlightenment is a Jihad, a struggle, and self-struggle
Against assumptions, foolishness, stupidity, social constructs
And lies

Enlightenment is a knowing an understanding
That what we think we know and understand to be true
Are only surface features, holo-images, shadows on a wall
Of what we believe to be real an important

Enlightenment is the illumination
Of social constructs, ideas and beliefs
Exposing them to the light of examination
And scrutiny, to understand that every
Religion is a man-made construction for a god
And what that god demands from his worshippers
Are only the creations of human imagination, bigotry, fears and
desire for control

Enlightenment is knowing

What is important in ones life and what is not

To understand that as we are living

We are also dying

And that which is important to us now

Tomorrow, will become a fading thing

To understand that we were not born

Jews, Christians, Muslims, etc.

But humankind, united in this creation and family

To be one people

Enlightenment is knowing that

There are no earthy religions for the dead

No earthy houses of worship for departed souls

To understand that religion is made for the living

All religions a god, but God has no religion

To understand these simple truths and apply it

In your life is the first step to enlightenment

"What earthy concerns are

Important to the dead?"

Darkness is the absents of light

Many walk about in darkness
Wondering around with no direction
No course to follow
Within them there is a nothingness, a void, emptiness
Their hearts are cold, no empathy
Their purpose for living is to pleasure themselves
Because they cannot feel for anyone else

They think they are on a straight path
But in truth they travel in circles
As a dog chasing its tail, moving in nowhere hurried motion
They are stuck in blind ignorance expecting change
Without changing

Darkness by nature is the absents of light
But light, by nature is an energetic force that illuminates
And drive darkness away
Light is a thing we must seek actively
And it is found only in knowledge
Knowledge that bring about change
Knowledge is light if that knowledge leads to
A higher state of understanding yourself
Those who walk in knowledge live expecting change
They are becoming aware

Ignorance is bliss, as the saying goes

And thus, the Garden of Eden was blissful ignorance

That is why after tasting knowledge

Man could not stay in paradise/ nor return to it

Because knowledge separates you from ignorance

Mystery of Mysteries

Mystery of mysteries, what can I know? What can I really know
of what waits for us in the grave.
What can I know of what is hidden from me?
If I were a preacher, I'm supposed to know and teach all about the
unknowns, these mysteries like I got the answers.
Like I know what I'm talking about.
But I don't.

I'm to teach you all about God and death, like I know about
God and death.
Let me tell you the truth, I never met God, though I suppose
To act like I have.
But the truth is, he is just someone that was taught to me as a child
and I grew up believing.
I believed in Santa Claus once too but I outgrew him. But if you
outgrow God you get thrown into hell.
That don't seem right.
But even though I feel like I know him after growing up believing all
these many decades, it doesn't change the truth, I have never seen
him or ever met.

Now death on the other hand is not shy about making herself known
at all. She's everywhere doing her thing.

She has no problem about coming right up to you and taking you out. But mystery of mysteries, where does she take you out to?

Now we preachers, prophets and palm readers claim to know what we really don't know. But to make that truth known would dry up the collection plates, donation boxes and bank accounts.
So during funerals we say what people want to believe:
"They've been taken to God" "He's crossed the river into paradise" "He has his mansion in the sky" "They're walking on streets of gold" "There is no more weeping and forever joy" "They are in gardens under watch rivers flow" "You can have your choice of Paradise virgins" and on and on and on.

Now Catholics love mystery and they don't even try to figure it out, and all the other religions do the same.
God is a mystery, we're told, and we're not ever to try to figure him out, because he's more than we can imagine or think.
No eye has seen or ear heard nor come into the imagination of man what God has prepared for us.

Now, I have to ask this question? If everything is supposed to be such a mystery, outside of our imagination, outside our knowledge of understanding, beyond what our eyes and ears could make sense of, then how in the hell can we mere mortals can be so detailed and sure about something we could never understand even if we did see it. I'm just sayin. It doesn't make sense.

Mother

For Effie (2/17/1984)

How shall I tell my love for thee
And how shall I express the fullness there-in?
For as the depths of the sea is a mystery
And the heights of the heavens unmeasurable
So great is my love for thee

Rickey K. Hood

Born in Charlotte, NC, Rickey K. Hood is an award-winning poet as well as an essayist, playwright and performer whose works have been featured in various national and international publications. He now resides in the DC Metro area, District Heights MD

www.ingramcontent.com/pod-product-compliance
Lightning Source LLC
La Vergne TN
LVHW011912080426
835508LV00007BA/488